The Conservative Government's Economic Record:
An End of Term Report

Nicholas Crafts
Professor of Economic History,
London School of Economics

Twenty-seventh Wincott Memorial Lecture delivered at
Bishop Partridge Hall, Church House, Westminster,
Tuesday, 14 October 1997

The Trustees of the IEA have agreed that any surplus
over costs arising from the sale of this Paper should be
donated to the Wincott Foundation

Published by the Institute of Economic Affairs for
The Wincott Foundation,1998

First published in March 1998 by
The Institute of Economic Affairs
2 Lord North Street
Westminster
London SW1P 3LB

© The Wincott Foundation 1998

Occasional Paper 104
All rights reserved
ISSN 0073-909X
ISBN 0-255 36413-X

Printed in Great Britain by
Hartington Fine Arts Limited, Lancing, West Sussex
Set in Times Roman 11 on 13 point

Contents

3

Tables

4

Foreword
LORD HARRIS OF HIGH CROSS

WITH SUPPORT FROM GRAHAM HUTTON AND LIONEL (LORD) ROBBINS, the directors of the IEA created the Wincott Foundation in 1969 to keep alive the memory and example of Harold Wincott, who by the time of this death in 1969 at the early age of 62 had become the undisputed doyen of post-war British financial journalism. His regular columns in the *Financial Times* were widely read for their combination of lucid writing, practical knowledge, shrewd judgement and fearless criticism based on the self-taught and timeless tenets of classical (non-party) liberalism.

Each year since 1970, in addition to conferring prestigious annual awards for journalists, the Trustees have invited an outstanding academic in the Wincott tradition, most commonly an economist, to lecture on a major issue of current (or neglected) public policy at home or abroad. With I think only one exception in 27 years, the texts have been published by the IEA as Occasional Papers (listed below, pages 43-45). Together they make a remarkable collection of scholarly commentaries by leading thinkers and a few practitioners on topics which, with very few exceptions, have retained interest and relevance for today's students and teachers.

For 1997 the lecturer chosen was Professor Nicholas Crafts who held the chairs in economic history at Leeds and Warwick before arriving at the LSE in 1995. His special study has been the analysis and measurement of economic development and growth, particularly in Britain and Europe, on which he is acknowledged as a foremost international authority. Particular attention will therefore be paid to this published version of a lecture delivered only a few months after the General Election had brought to an end a period of Conservative government which had set out 18 years earlier to halt and reverse Britain's century-long, relative economic decline.

The natural impulse of an impatient student might be to turn eagerly to the Tables which certainly provide a marvellously concise selection and summary of the Tory record in bald macro-economic statistics of GDP, investment, inflation, unemployment and the rest. But for old IEA-watchers who are at least a little wary of such precise-looking national aggregates, I strongly commend running quickly through the text first before going back to re-read it more carefully and dwelling longer on each set of figures.

I recall an early IEA Trustee, the sage Professor John Jewkes of Oxford University, who used to warn against the prevailing over-reliance on figures for the simple reason that they omitted factors and forces which did not lend themselves easily to measurement. The briefest reading of the text will go far to exonerate our cautious, level-headed author of such pitfalls. Having lived through the period of 'growthmanship' in the 1960s and 1970s when economists who should have know better vied with one another to urge almost indiscriminate 'investment' as the engine of economic progress, I particularly welcomed Professor Crafts's emphasis on its quality as measured by increasingly competitive markets in the 1980s, rather than its crude quantity.

That distinction was at the forefront of Harold Wincott's unwavering criticism of inflationary public finance, bloated nationalised industries, trade union restrictionism, high taxation of profits and other impediments to efficient production, all of which 'Thatcherism' took courage to tackle – with impressive, if mixed, results that the author judiciously appraises.

However, one valuable by-product of macro-measurement is to suggest unexpected outcomes which in turn provoke sharp questions for further investigation. I suspect Wincott would have shared my surprise at Table 6, which suggests that the service sector lagged so far behind the dramatic improvement in labour productivity in manufacturing. In his time, before BT swept away the old antique GPO, businesses would wait weeks if not months for the installation of a new telephone line, just as shops and pubs opened to suit the comfort of employees rather than the convenience of customers. Can the macro-economist's precise-looking statistics ever fully capture such improvements in quality of service and choice which are likely to form an increasing part of standards of living in ever more prosperous societies? And what about the growing contribution to economic welfare from the informal or underground economy which largely escapes measurement?

It is one indication of the value of this lively, wide-ranging contribution to contemporary British history that it will long continue to stimulate debate from which we can hope for the better economic understanding which it is the purpose of both the Wincott Foundation and the IEA to advance. In commending this Occasional Paper for wider study and discussion, the Trustees, Directors and the Advisers emphasise that authors are encouraged to draw their own conclusions from their analysis without committing the IEA, which as an educational charity has no corporate views.

March 1998   RALPH HARRIS
Chairman of Trustees,
The Wincott Foundation

The Author

NICHOLAS CRAFTS has been Professor of Economic History at the London School of Economics since 1995. Previously he was Fellow and Praelector in Economics at University College, Oxford (1977-86), Professor of Economic History at the University of Leeds (1987-88), and Professor of Economic History at the University of Warwick (1988-95).

He was born in 1949 and educated at Brunts Grammar School, Mansfield, and Trinity College, Cambridge. His publications include *Britain's Relative Economic Decline, 1870-1995* (1997), and articles in many journals including *Economic History Review, Economic Journal, Journal of Economic History,* and *Journal of Economic Perspectives*. He has recently edited and contributed to *Economic Growth in Europe since 1945* (1996) (with Gianni Toniolo). He is a member of the Council of the Economic History Society and is a Fellow of the British Academy (elected 1992).

For the IEA Professor Crafts has previously contributed *Can De-Industrialisation Seriously Damage Your Wealth?* (Hobart Paper No. 120, 1993).

The Conservative Government's Economic Record: An End of Term Report
NICHOLAS CRAFTS

1. Introduction

EIGHTEEN YEARS OF CONSERVATIVE GOVERNMENTS ended on 1 May 1997 with a landslide defeat. This is an opportune moment to appraise economic policy under the Conservatives with a view both to assessing their performance and also to highlighting lessons for 'New Labour'. The focus of this lecture is selective and concentrates on macro-economic issues – growth, inflation and unemployment – and above all on examining the progress made in the central task of reversing relative economic decline.

At least in the first half of the period, Thatcherite convictions promoted a phase of radical reform which entailed a substantial departure from the approach of all governments in the earlier post-war years. The post-war settlement was abandoned and Keynesianism was repudiated. A new emphasis on the supply side addressed weak productivity performance and labour market failures. The disarray of the left and the Falklands War provided a rare opportunity to give the long term more than usual weight. Yet, both the policy mix and its subsequent results were heavily influenced by the unfortunate legacy of the 1960s and 1970s and, as always, radicalism was tempered by the need to get re-elected.

Moreover, the establishment of a satisfactory framework for short-term macro-economic management remained problematic throughout and failures in this area eventually undermined the Conservatives' reputation for economic competence. The 1990s thus became an unhappy time in which ensuring survival of the government limited the scope for pressing on with a radical agenda. Yet, in these years, favourable comparisons of British economic performance relative to our European peer group became increasingly frequent and, despite the rhetoric of opposition, the incoming government has clearly accepted the main thrust of the supply-side reforms introduced under the Conservatives.

Against this background, the lecture attempts the following:

- to set out in comparative perspective the raw data on key macro-economic objectives;
- to consider the design of policy in the light of modern economic theory;
- to assess the overall macro-economic impact of the supply-side reforms.

This will provide key ingredients for those who want to judge the Conservatives' record. On this, however, opinions will differ and I have no wish to assert my own view. Three specific reasons for this caution are, *first*, that the counterfactual of what would have happened with an alternative policy stance is not observable; *second*, that assessment of the political constraints on what was feasible is beyond my expertise; *third*, and most important, that an overall view depends on value-judgements on the relative weight given to different policy objectives on which there is no consensus.

2. A Comparative Overview of Macro-economic Performance

THIS SECTION PROVIDES A BRIEF SUMMARY of Britain's track record with regard to levels of real GDP per person, growth, inflation and unemployment rates. Relative economic decline occurs where growth is slower than in other countries with the long-term result that, although real income increases in absolute terms, it falls relative to a peer group of countries. The Tables are constructed to permit comparisons both with other European and G7 countries and also with the British experience before 1979.

Tables 1 and 2 report comparisons of growth rates and their corollary in terms of league tables of real output per person. Real GDP is measured in terms of purchasing power parity adjusted dollars. Tables 1 and 2 show clearly that the years between 1950 and 1979 were a period of substantial relative economic decline. The UK fell from third to 11th among these countries in terms of real GDP per person and had the equal lowest growth rate. Between 1979 and 1996, the UK dropped one more place to 12th in real GDP per person and attained an about average growth rate. This took place in the context of a widespread retardation in growth in which British growth did not accelerate but slowed a lot less than most.

10

Table 1: Real GDP per Person (in international purchasing power parity adjusted dollars, 1990)

	1950		1979		1996	
1.	USA	9,617	USA	18,574	USA	23,719
2.	Switzerland	8,939	Switzerland	17,800	Norway	22,256
3.	UK	6,847	W. Germany	15,257	Switzerland	20,262
4.	Sweden	6,738	France	14,850	Denmark	19,803
5.	Denmark	6,683	Denmark	14,731	W. Germany	19,622
6.	Netherlands	5,850	Sweden	14,720	Japan	19,582
7.	Norway	5,403	Netherlands	14,317	Netherlands	18,504
8.	Belgium	5,346	Norway	14,280	France	18,207
9.	France	5,221	Austria	13,487	Austria	17,951
10.	W. Germany	4,281	Belgium	13,457	Belgium	17,756
11.	Finland	4,131	UK	13,087	Sweden	17,566
12.	Austria	3,731	Japan	12,754	UK	17,326
13.	Italy	3,425	Italy	12,588	Italy	16,814
14.	Ireland	3,325	Finland	12,089	Finland	15,864
15.	Spain	2,397	Spain	9,488	Ireland	15,820
16.	Japan	1,873	Ireland	7,712	Spain	13,132

Sources: Maddison (1995, 1997) supplemented for West Germany in 1996 by GDP from IFO (1997) and by population from Statistisches Bundesamt (1997).

Table 2: Growth of Real GDP per Person, 1950-1996
(per cent)

1950-79		*1979-96*	
USA	2·3	USA	1·5
Switzerland	2·4	Switzerland	0·8
UK	2·3	West Germany	1·5
Sweden	3·2	France	1·2
Denmark	2·8	Denmark	1·8
Netherlands	3·1	Sweden	1·0
Norway	3·4	Netherlands	1·5
Belgium	4·5	Norway	2·6
France	3·8	Austria	1·7
West Germany	4·5	Belgium	1·7
Finland	3·8	UK	1·7
Austria	4·5	Japan	2·6
Italy	4·6	Italy	1·7
Ireland	2·9	Finland	1·6
Spain	4·8	Spain	1·9
Japan	6·8	Ireland	4·3

Sources: as for Table 1.

Table 3 sets out estimates of unemployment rates. These are based on an internationally and inter-temporally standardised definition which, for the present-day UK, gives a figure above that of the claimant count which is quoted as the 'headline rate' each month. Clearly, throughout the Conservative years, unemployment was much higher than in the earlier period. Unemployment rates rose in every country in 1980-1995 compared with 1955-1979 but the increase in the UK was larger than most. Moreover, the UK had above-average unemployment both before and after 1979. On the other hand, by 1996 British unemployment was lower than that in other large European countries and this was not wholly attributable to differences in the business cycle.

Comparisons of inflation are given in Table 4. The high inflation of the 1970s fell markedly in the 1980s and the 1990s saw Britain return to the relatively low inflation rates of the mid-1960s. This was by no means outstanding in comparative terms – indeed, it is

Table 3: Average Rates of Standardised Unemployment (per cent)

1955-79		1980-95		1996	
Norway	0·3	Switzerland	2·1	Japan	3·4
Switzerland	0·5	Japan	2·5	Switzerland	3·5
Sweden	1·6	Norway	3·8	Austria	4·4
Austria	1·7	Sweden	4·1	Norway	4·9
Japan	1·7	Austria	4·4	USA	5·4
Germany	1·8	Germany	6·1	Denmark	6·0
Netherlands	2·4	USA	6·9	Netherlands	6·3
Finland	2·5	Italy	7·5	UK	8·2
France	2·5	Finland	7·8	Germany	9·0
Spain	3·1	Netherlands	8·6	Italy	9·5
Denmark	3·2	France	9·6	Belgium	9·8
UK	3·3	Denmark	9·7	Sweden	10·0
Belgium	3·5	UK	9·7	Ireland	12·3
Italy	4·7	Belgium	9·8	France	12·4
USA	5·3	Ireland	14·1	Finland	15·7
Ireland	5·9	Spain	18·4	Spain	22·2

Sources: Layard *et al.* (1994) updated using OECD (1997b).

very similar to the outcome in the other countries with double-digit inflation in the 1970s. The disappearance of the commodity price shocks of the 1970s and the widespread changes in policy priorities to which inflation gave rise have combined to transform expectations. In each period, however, Britain had above-average inflation and was actually third worst (after Italy and Spain) in 1990-1996.

3. Developments in Economic Theory

WHILE THE CONSERVATIVES WERE RESHAPING British economic policy, key ideas in economics were also undergoing substantial revision. A verdict on their economic stewardship informed by today's economic theory will be very different from one based on the ideas of the 1970s. This section offers an outline of some of the most relevant developments.

13

Table 4: Average Rates of Inflation (per cent)

1970-79		*1980-89*		*1990-96*	
Germany	5·3	Japan	2·2	Japan	1·0
Switzerland	5·3	Netherlands	2·3	Ireland	1·5
Austria	6·5	Germany	2·9	Denmark	2·0
USA	6·8	Switzerland	3·9	Netherlands	2·0
Belgium	7·5	Austria	4·1	France	2·2
Norway	7·8	Belgium	4·6	Norway	2·2
Netherlands	7·9	USA	5·0	Finland	2·3
Japan	8·1	Denmark	6·3	Belgium	2·7
Sweden	9·4	France	7·2	Switzerland	2·9
France	9·7	Norway	7·2	USA	2·9
Denmark	9·9	Finland	7·5	Germany	3·1
Finland	11·6	UK	7·5	Austria	3·2
UK	13·4	Sweden	8·1	Sweden	3·9
Ireland	13·7	Ireland	8·7	UK	4·0
Italy	14·4	Spain	10·1	Italy	5·3
Spain	15·3	Italy	12·0	Spain	5·4

Source: OECD (1997a) based on GDP deflators.

New Growth Economics

Growth economics has been transformed in the last 10 years or so. The following brief synopsis draws heavily on an earlier survey in which more detail is provided (Crafts, 1996). The central thrust of recent theorising places productivity growth at the heart of the growth process and regards technological change rather than investment in ever more of the same capital goods as the key to sustaining long-run growth. As in traditional neo-classical growth theory, routine investment, whether in human or physical capital, runs into diminishing returns. Innovation, whether in the form of initial invention or through technology transfer, is seen as motivated by profit and is modelled as endogenous whereas in traditional growth economics it was unexplained. It follows that incentive structures are central to the supply of cost-reducing effort, and thus to the growth process. These should be the focal point of policies, which will be primarily micro-economic, to promote growth.

This suggests that it is useful to distinguish between three different levels of explanation for growth outcomes and prospects. *First*, the proximate sources of growth can be identified in terms of the growth of factor inputs and productivity which reflect investment rates, skill formation, innovative activity, and so on. *Second*, the underlying reasons for the behaviour of these variables in terms of actions by managers and workers and the ways in which institutions and government policy affect them can be considered. *Third*, the fundamentals which sustain the decisions of key agents both in politics and in business can be explored through the pursuit of votes and profits.

Productivity growth tends to be fastest during phases of catch-up when countries are reducing the productivity gap with the leader(s) by emulating some of its technological and organisational advances and moving towards its levels of capital per person. When the catch-up phase peters out, returns to investment fall and growth slows down; in most of Western Europe this happened during the 1970s (Crafts and Toniolo, 1996). For post-catch-up economies, growth at 2-3 per cent per year is about as good as it gets.

Central among the factors that influence efforts to raise productivity is the expectation of profit and thus the ability to appropriate returns from successful ventures. Given the large element of sunk costs involved, exposure to ex-post opportunism ('hold-up') will reduce innovative activity and this means that a wide variety of micro-economic arrangements can affect the growth rate, including relationships between shareholders and managers and between firms and trade unions. Fiscal policy will also have an impact on growth – expenditure on infrastructure tends to raise returns to private sector investment while taxation does the opposite. As the total size of the government budget increases relative to GDP, the negative effect eventually outweighs the positive, as seems generally to be the case in OECD countries (Dowrick, 1996).

A notable feature of many supply-side policies that will raise productivity growth is that their pay-off is in the long term though the costs are felt more immediately while the identity of the gainers and losers is uncertain. In such cases, since it is not usually possible

15

for politicians credibly to promise that losers will be compensated, those who fear that they will lose may form a majority who rationally oppose beneficial changes and policy may exhibit a 'status-quo bias' (Fernandez and Rodrik, 1991). Alternatively, as with the closure of sunset industries, it may be that gains exceed losses from change but the former are spread very thinly over many voters while the latter are concentrated such that there are votes to be lost but none to be gained. Thus, it may often be politically rational not to implement reforms that are good for growth.

Equilibrium Unemployment

During the 1980s it became normal to analyse the labour market in terms of price and wage setting by firms and workers in an imperfectly competitive framework. The equilibrium concept in this approach, which argues that there is no long-run trade-off between inflation and unemployment, is the NAIRU (Non-Accelerating Inflation Rate of Unemployment). The level of the NAIRU depends on structural features of the labour market and attempts to reduce unemployment below this level through stimulating aggregate demand lead ultimately to inflation rather than sustained reductions in unemployment. A detailed account of this work and an assessment of the empirical evidence can be found in Bean (1994), on which this section has drawn.

The major influences on the NAIRU, and thus the potential levers on which policy can operate to affect equilibrium unemployment, are wage-bargaining systems, the duration and generosity of unemployment benefits, mismatch in skills and/or location between labour supply and demand, and the size of the tax wedge between the real wage paid by employers and that received by workers. In general, trends in all of these variables were unfavourable in OECD countries during the 1970s and early 1980s and estimated NAIRUs tended to rise sharply. Nevertheless, the magnitude and persistence of the increases were greater than might have been expected.

An important additional pressure on the labour market in OECD countries since the mid-1970s has come from technological change. In general, the process of economic growth involves 'creative destruction' as new products and processes are discovered and old ones are superseded. There is no reason to suppose that

16

technological change or rapid productivity growth *per se* promote unemployment, although there will be impacts on the composition of employment and equilibrium wage differentials. In fact, a key aspect of recent experience has been a strong bias in technological change towards saving unskilled labour with the result that the demand for this type of labour has fallen relative to supply, especially in countries with relatively low levels of skill formation where the required wage flexibility to absorb this unskilled labour is particularly high (Nickell and Bell, 1996).

The extent to which government can counter adverse trends in equilibrium unemployment is another area of policy where *status quo* bias is to be expected. In general, seeking to reduce equilibrium unemployment through raising the flexibility of labour markets is likely to create both gainers and losers. The gainers will tend to be skilled workers whose productivity and wages will be enhanced by the employment of additional unskilled colleagues and the unemployed with the worst prospects of getting a job prior to the reform who may now be priced into a job. The losers will be the unskilled and those who would probably have been employed soon anyway because their expected wages will have fallen. It is not surprising that an analysis of the composition of the labour force suggests that *status quo* bias is likely to be a serious obstacle to labour market de-regulation in many European countries (Alogoskoufis *et al.*, 1995).

Discretion vs Rules in Macro-economic Policy

The explicit recognition of the time inconsistency problem in the late 1970s overturned the previous presumption in favour of discretion in macro-economic policy-making and renewed interest in devising appropriate rules to counter the inflationary bias that is predicted when the government is unable to commit itself not to inflate. Developments in the analysis of these topics are well reviewed in the context of British monetary policy-making in Haldane (1995), on which this section draws.

Inflationary bias arises when policy-makers have discretion because there is always a temptation in the pursuit of votes to create a short-term boom resulting in an initial fall in unemployment at the expense of higher inflation later. Knowing this, the private sector realises that promises not to do this are not credible and factors the expected inflation into its expectations. The eventual outcome is anticipated inflation but no output or employment gain. A pre-commitment to a policy rule is a possible solution to this problem of inflationary bias and the 19th-century Gold Standard fulfilled this rôle (Bordo and Kydland, 1995). An alternative may be to delegate policy to an independent central bank with an appropriately designed contract and there is evidence to suggest that, under floating exchange rates, this leads to lower inflation (Alesina and Summers, 1993).

A disadvantage of credible rules is in terms of reduced policy flexibility in the face of recessionary shocks and an associated risk of high output losses. Staying on the Gold Standard in the 1930s implied a much more severe depression and slower recovery than was the case for those countries (like the UK) which left or were forced out quickly (Eichengreen and Sachs, 1985). It may be possible to counter this, at least to some extent, in the case of delegating policy to an independent central bank through contingency clauses or careful design of rewards and penalties for the bank. When a fixed exchange rate is used as the rule, it may be harder to guard against the deflationary risks of limiting discretion.

The choice between a fixed exchange rate and delegating monetary authority to an independent central bank also has implications for the availability of policy instruments for domestic aggregate demand management. As is well-known from standard Mundell-Fleming analysis, a fixed exchange rate means that the interest rate weapon is forgone and fiscal policy must be used. Conversely, under floating rates monetary policy sovereignty is retained and interest rates can be used but fiscal policy is ineffective since its impact is negated by changes in the exchange rate.

In the case of big increases of import prices of the kind experienced in the 1970s, the choices facing the governments (or central banks) are necessarily very unpleasant. In general, it is likely that it will be optimal to accommodate the inflationary shock, at least to some extent. Indeed, even in countries like Germany where credible policy pre-commitment had been achieved, inflation was allowed to rise somewhat. Over time, therefore, judgements on the success of alternative counter-inflationary frameworks need to allow for external circumstances.

4. The Legacy in 1979

INTERNATIONAL COMPARISONS SHOW that economic performance was seriously disappointing from the 1950s through the 1970s. In part, this stemmed from mistaken economic policies and institutional deficiencies which had to be corrected if relative economic decline was to cease or be reversed. The quality of the capital stock and the labour force and productivity levels in 1979 reflected these problems as did macro-economic indicators like inflation and unemployment. Moreover, the legacy of these decades also shaped the options open to the incoming government. Assessments of the Conservatives' economic record must take account of the starting point.

From the early 1960s there had been a great deal of policy experimentation aimed at promoting faster economic growth. Surprisingly to modern eyes, policy did not focus effectively on addressing market failures in human capital formation or the diffusion of technological knowledge or on sharpening the incentives for effort in pursuit of cost-reductions. Instead, the thrust of policy was to subsidise physical capital, to run significant parts of the economy under state ownership, to promote 'national champion' firms and prestige research projects while failing to implement satisfactory reforms of either industrial relations or taxation. To some extent, similar policy errors were ,made throughout Europe but overall the damage done in Britain was relatively high (Crafts, 1997, pp. 45-46).

In some ways, earlier failures create favourable opportunities. Thus, a belated catch-up might allow relatively rapid productivity growth for a while, as has happened recently in Ireland. Also, it was easier for the British to believe that the post-war settlement was outmoded than was generally the case elsewhere in Europe. On the other hand, future outcomes and policy options might be seriously constrained by inherited weaknesses.

For example, there is widespread agreement that vocational training left a lot to be desired. Unlike countries such as Germany, Britain did not develop a set of (corporatist) institutions centred on internal labour markets and employers' organisations to make it worth while for juveniles to train and to mitigate poaching problems (Soskice, 1994). This mattered not only for productivity growth but also meant that future adjustment problems arising from biased technological change were exacerbated. In 1979, only 23 per cent of the British labour force held intermediate qualifications compared with 61 per cent in Germany (Steedman, 1990), while cross-section studies of British and German manufacturing have shown that there was a substantial correlation between the vocational qualifications gap and the productivity gap (O'Mahony and Wagner, 1994).

Inefficient use of labour was a common complaint against British industry in the 1960s and 1970s.This clearly played a large part in the much remarked productivity gap between British manufacturing and its European peer group. A shake-out of this under-employed labour would be an inherent part of future reductions in the productivity shortfall but would also imply additional adjustment problems in the labour market and the possibility of increased structural unemployment. Moreover, it also implied that appreciable increases in the real exchange rate would lead to a very rapid de-industrialisation of the labour force.

Overstaffing was frequently attributed to management failure – for example, in 21 out of 23 cases reviewed by Pratten and Atkinson (1976). British managers had inferior qualifications relative particularly to their American counterparts (Broadberry and Wagner, 1996). It is also true that they operated in a capital market which was rather inefficient in disciplining bad management but which skewed incentives to use large amounts of top management time in pursuing, pre-empting or defending takeovers (Singh, 1975). Nevertheless, it should be recognised that the low-effort equilibrium characteristic of many sectors reflected deals made between firms and their workers and thus the bargaining environment rather than simply management failure. Changes both in bargaining structures and in bargaining power would have productivity implications.

Britain was an outlier in terms of industrial relations – the only case in Europe of powerful, long-established but de-centralised trade unionism (Crouch, 1993). This had implications for productivity growth as well as for the NAIRU. Prais (1981) provided detailed case-study evidence for the 1960s and 1970s which showed that in six out of 10 industries that he investigated (brewing, metal boxes, motor vehicles, newspapers, tobacco and tyres), increases in productivity had been retarded by problems of

20

negotiating appropriate staffing levels when technology improved. The inability of workers to commit themselves to good behaviour was an obstacle to investment and multiple unionism in particular appears to have been associated with reduced productivity growth (Bean and Crafts, 1996).

The traditional pattern of British industrial relations sustained wage bargaining arrangements that were not conducive to a low equilibrium level of unemployment, in particular combining low levels of co-ordination of both employers and unions with a high coverage of the workforce by collective bargaining agreements (Layard *et al.*, 1994). Successive governments in the 1960s and 1970s tried to suppress the problem through incomes policies but these were ultimately incapable of preventing a large rise in equilibrium unemployment. Increasing wage militancy on the part of unions was augmented by rising unemployment benefits and increased labour taxes in pushing up the NAIRU (Layard and Nickell, 1985).

Against a background of a rising NAIRU and commodity price shocks, the 1970s were characterised in Britain as elsewhere in the OECD by stagflation. By the mid-1970s, policy was being conducted almost entirely on the basis of discretion rather than rules following the collapse of the Bretton Woods exchange rate system. The Bank of England had been nationalised in 1946 and was certainly not independent of government. This contrasted markedly with the position of the Bundesbank which delivered a relatively low level of inflation in Germany through the external shocks of the 1970s.

The 1960s and 1970s were a period of high profile macro-economic policy when the pursuit of short-run macro-economic objectives frequently took precedence over supply-side considerations. It was widely believed that Keynesian policies could ensure low levels of unemployment and that voters would severely punish governments which failed to achieve this through discretionary policy. At the same time, policy-makers were persistently worried that, in tight labour markets, the collective bargaining system would promote high wage inflation. The implication was a continuing series of efforts to arrive at agreements between the government and organised labour to obtain wage restraint in exchange for other policy commitments. This

21

culminated in the so-called 'Social Contract' of the mid-1970s which exposed very clearly the constraints that macro-economic pressures put on supply-side policy through the interventionist industrial policies that were encouraged and the reforms of taxation and industrial relations that were precluded.

Given the weaknesses of the late-1970s British economy, disengaging from this approach to macro-economic policy and re-orientating supply-side policy could be expected at best to entail substantial short-term pain with a hope of long-term gain only if the reforms could be sustained for a prolonged period. This was not a situation susceptible of a quick cure.

5. The Design of the Thatcher Experiment

THE THATCHER YEARS ARE widely recognised to have been a period of radical reform during which the earlier post-war consensus was abandoned. The earlier priority given to full employment and reducing inequality of income distribution was dropped in favour of controlling inflation and promoting productivity growth. The government sought to escape the trade unions' veto on economic reform and many of the policy changes of the 1980s would have been regarded as inconceivable by informed opinion in the 1960s and 1970s – for example, the reduction of the top marginal income tax rate to 40 per cent, the privatisation of the public utilities and the decimation of the NUM. Although the subsequent Major period reflected a different style of government, nevertheless the Thatcher experiment was refined and extended rather than abandoned.

This section considers the design of the policy innovations that were directed at raising the rate of economic growth and reducing unemployment and inflation. In doing so, it will both place them in the context of the recent developments in economic theory noted in Section 3 and also examine the extent to which earlier failures were addressed. A review of evidence on the results of the reforms follows in Section 6.

Promoting Productivity Improvement

The thrust of policy was to strengthen incentives and market disciplines rather than to subsidise physical investment. Among the key elements of the new supply-side policy were privatisation and deregulation, reform of industrial relations, restructuring of taxation and restraint on the growth of public expenditure, radical revision of vocational training and expansion of higher education. Foreign direct investment was encouraged and rapid de-industrialisation was accepted and accompanied by a sharp reduction in subsidies to troubled industries. Indirectly, other policies also had effects, in particular those which impacted on effort bargains.

In broad outline, this re-orientation of policy both has some support from modern growth economics and also remedied earlier mistakes. Errors were more of omission and incompleteness than of misdirection. Both privatisation with RPI-X regulation and the changes in industrial relations – end of the closed shop, decline in multiple unionism, reduced workers' bargaining power – can be seen as raising managers' incentives to innovate and to raise productivity. Subsidies to physical investment are not justified in general by an excess of social over private returns (Oulton and Young, 1996). Openness is positively related to productivity growth through stimulating technology transfer and forcing managers to concentrate on cost reduction rather than rent-seeking (Edwards, 1997). Reductions in marginal direct tax rates and improved supply of human capital can also raise the returns to innovative effort.

Nevertheless, there were, clearly, a number of weaknesses in the implementation of this approach which may be expected to have reduced its effectiveness. *First*, it is clear that, although privatisation encouraged cost-reduction and the regulatory régime was an improvement over American-style rate-of-return regulation, some of the possible productivity gains were forgone through failures to introduce competition – for example, British Gas – and to set X factors high enough – for instance, British Telecom (Vickers and Yarrow, 1988).

Second, given that in the context of principal-agent problems within firms we can generally expect competition to encourage endogenous innovation (Aghion and Howitt, 1997), the government's lack of interest in strengthening anti-trust policy must be seen as disappointing (Williams, 1993).

Third, despite the government's rhetoric, progress in reducing the burden of taxation on growth was not pursued with any great vigour, especially during the 1990s. Certainly, the earlier rapid rise

23

in government spending as a proportion of GDP ceased after the mid-1970s and, as Table 5 indicates, this ratio fell well behind the big-spending European countries by the 1990s. Also, the very high marginal direct tax rates were abolished and VAT was increased. Nevertheless, both VAT revenues relative to GDP and the VAT tax base are low by European standards (Owens and Whitehouse, 1996).

Similarly, in 1980 the government exhibited considerable courage in ending the indexing of benefits to earnings and linking them instead to prices. By the mid-1990s, this implied a saving of over 3 per cent of GDP and over £7 billion on pensions alone (Tyrie, 1996, p. 22). More radical schemes to restructure welfare were, however, regarded as 'too difficult' despite clear evidence that benefits like the basic state pension and, especially, child benefit were very poorly targeted at the poor. An opportunity both to enhance provision for the seriously needy and to reduce the burden of taxation at the same time was neglected (Dilnot et al., 1984).

Reducing Unemployment

Keynesian responses to unemployment were eschewed by the Conservatives, most famously in the Budget of 1981 when 364 economists indicated their disapproval. Policy focussed on reducing the NAIRU. The main leverage initially was sought through reducing taxes on labour, weakening trade unions and promoting reform of collective bargaining agreements, together with reductions in benefits relative to wages. In the late 1980s, unemployment benefit regulations were tightened significantly. From 1986, this was complemented by increased attention to reform of education and training which can be seen as attempting to address structural unemployment by raising the stock of skills in the labour force.

Empirical research in the NAIRU tradition finds that high unemployment is associated with generous unemployment benefits that continue indefinitely with little pressure to take work, high coverage of collective bargaining with no co-ordination between employers or unions, high overall taxes and poor educational standards at the bottom of the labour market (Nickell, 1997, p. 72). Thus, well-defined interventions along these lines should have

Table 5: Government Current Disbursements (as per cent of GDP)

1960-73		1974-79		1980-89		1990-95	
Japan	14·0	Japan	21·7	Japan	26·4	Japan	26·8
Spain	16·4	Spain	23·6	Switzerland	30·3	Switzerland	34·4
Switzerland	20·3	Switzerland	29·2	Spain	34·3	USA	34·6
Finland	25·6	USA	31·1	USA	34·4	Spain	40·2
USA	27·2	Finland	34·3	Finland	39·5	Ireland	40·8
Denmark	29·3	Italy	38·7	UK	41·9	UK	40·9
Ireland	29·3	France	39·3	Germany	43·8	Germany	44·4
Italy	30·0	UK	39·7	Italy	44·5	Austria	47·1
UK	31·8	Austria	40·0	Austria	45·3	France	48·8
Austria	31·9	Ireland	40·0	Norway	46·1	Italy	50·6
Germany	31·9	Germany	42·2	France	46·7	Norway	51·0
Norway	32·5	Norway	43·7	Ireland	47·4	Belgium	53·8
Sweden	33·2	Denmark	44·6	Denmark	56·0	Netherlands	53·9
France	33·7	Belgium	48·0	Netherlands	56·3	Finland	54·0
Belgium	34·9	Netherlands	49·1	Belgium	57·4	Denmark	59·2
Netherlands	35·3	Sweden	49·5	Sweden	59·2	Sweden	63·5

Sources: OECD (1996a, 1997a).

reduced equilibrium unemployment. Given the implications of the Social Contract for no-go areas in supply-side policy, it is not surprising that incomes policies were abandoned and the alternative of seeking to establish greater co-ordination in wage bargaining was not pursued.

Much less commendable was the complementary approach of trying to hide unemployment both by changing the basis on which it was counted and by encouraging re-location into categories such as disability and youth training. As is well-known, a fall in the labour force relative to employment raises wage pressure just as much as a rise in employment relative to the labour force – thus the long-run effect of such measures is to reduce real GDP per person rather than to reduce the unemployment rate (Nickell, 1997, pp. 70-71).

Counter-Inflationary Policy

In macro-economic policy, the central feature was retreat from discretionary demand management. The Medium-Term Financial Strategy (MTFS) sought to put policy on the basis of pre-announced monetary targets and both fiscal and monetary adjustments now responded to inflation rather than unemployment. The immediate implication of the MTFS was a tightening of policy which precipitated a severe recession and a big jump in the exchange rate (Britton, 1991). Difficulties in the control and interpretation of monetary targets led by 1986 to the adoption of an informal exchange rate target and then, from 1990 to 1992, to membership of ERM. After 1992, inflation targets were adopted together with a greater transparency in policy formulation and in Bank of England monitoring of inflationary pressures.

Counter-inflationary policy, at least up to 1992, was clearly much less well-conceived than either labour market or supply-side policy, although this was not the general perception during the first two Thatcher governments where disinflation was praised but the consequences for the real economy frequently deplored. Two big problems loom large – the failure to choose suitable policy targets and the reluctance to surrender political control of monetary and/or exchange rate policy.

Neither M3 nor a fixed DM/£ rate appeals as a good nominal anchor for policy: both appear inferior to the inflation targets eventually adopted after 1992. The first is unsatisfactory because it is hard to control and its relation to inflation is often difficult to predict. The second is not satisfactory because the appropriate stances of monetary policy in Germany and Britain may differ substantially, and the emphasis it places on the use of fiscal policy as a stabiliser seems inconsistent with the government's professed aim of setting taxes on micro-economic/supply-side criteria.

It is indeed difficult to believe that an independent central bank with a (Walsh) contract based on an inflation target could possibly have presided over the Lawson boom and subsequent bust. This seems to have been largely an unnecessary and self-inflicted wound and the contrast at this point with developments in New Zealand where the central bank was made independent with what appear to have been well-designed incentives is striking (Walsh, 1995).

6. The Impact of the Reforms on the Real Economy

THIS SECTION COMPLEMENTS THE ANALYSIS of Section 5 by reviewing quantitative estimates from the literature on the impact of the Conservatives' reforms on productivity performance and unemployment. The state of knowledge does not, of course, permit a complete decomposition of the observed changes or a full comparison with a do-nothing policy still less relative to alternative policy packages. Nevertheless, it is possible to identify some likely effects of the policy innovations.

Productivity Performance

The striking feature of this period was the strong upturn in labour productivity growth in manufacturing. This had only a muted impact on the economy overall because it was not accompanied by faster productivity growth in the services sector, as is shown in Table 6, which suggests that the reforms had their strongest impact in manufacturing where levels of productivity relative to leading European countries had fallen back spectacularly in the previous 30 years.

Table 7 reports estimates on a purchasing power parity basis that show a substantial reduction in manufacturing productivity gaps between the UK and other countries between 1979 and 1995 when Britain's relative position was generally rather better than in 1973.

Table 6: Growth of UK Labour Productivity
(per cent per year)

	1960-79	*1979-96*
Whole Economy	2·4	2·6
Manufacturing	1·9	3·6

Source: ONS (1997).

This appears not to be the case for marketed services which account for a much larger share of employment in Britain than manufacturing. The early 1980s saw massive job-shedding in British manufacturing which raised capital per remaining worker,

Table 7: Relative Productivity in Manufacturing and Marketed Services
(UK = 100 in each year)

Manufacturing

	1950	*1973*	*1979*	*1995*
France	90·4	130·6	149·1	122·1
Japan	45·2	90·5	113·8	104·4
USA	245·7	186·6	179·9	143·5
West Germany	97·5	142·0	163·7	116·8

Marketed Services

France	n.a.	132·3	143·2	136·0
USA	n.a.	156·9	150·3	137·8
West Germany	n.a	100·6	115·4	133·5

Sources: For manufacturing, Pilat (1996) extended to 1950 and interpolated to 1979 using van Ark (1993), and for services, O'Mahony *et al*. (1996). Please note that the Pilat figures are comparisons between the other countries and the USA and were originally expressed using the USA as the base country. The final year for the services comparison is 1993 not 1995. Productivity is measured as value-added per hour worked.

but an analysis of Anglo-German productivity levels also found that a substantial increase in total factor productivity (TFP) accounted for about half the decline in the labour productivity gap between 1979 and 1989 (O'Mahony and Wagner, 1994).

A major impact on productivity in the manufacturing sector seems to have come from changes in the bargaining environment and associated developments in industrial relations. Rising unemployment in the early 1980s and increased competitive pressures from imports became less favourable to the exercise of union power and to low-effort equilibria. This was clearly associated with at least once-and-for-all improvements in labour productivity as a whole host of econometric studies show (Bean and Symons, 1989; Haskel, 1991; Nickell *et al.*, 1992). Moreover, negative effects of union recognition on investment (Denny and Nickell, 1992) and of multiple unionism on TFP growth (Bean and Crafts, 1996) are found to be much reduced and to disappear respectively.

Given the prevailing widespread inefficiency of labour use, the recessionary shock of the early 1980s exacerbated by the ill-judged monetary policy of the time had a silver lining in terms of better productivity through the shake-out of labour and change in bargaining power that it precipitated. This should not be taken to mean that recessions are generally good for growth. On the contrary, cross-sectional econometric evidence suggests that trend growth in the UK could rise by over 0·5 per cent per year if it achieves greater macro-economic stability in future (Oulton, 1995).

European comparisons suggest that product market deregulation (including privatisation) was strongly correlated with better productivity performance over 1980-94 and this may have given the UK a gain of around 0·6 percentage points per year in TFP growth relative to the average EU member-state where de-regulation proceeded much more slowly (Koedijk and Kremers, 1996). Studies have concluded that the prospect and arrival of privatisation stimulated productivity growth on average (Bishop and Thompson, 1992; Parker and Martin, 1995), and a detailed study of electricity generation concluded that the present value of the net benefits was equal to a cost saving of 5 per cent for ever, mostly through improved operating efficiency (Newbery and Pollitt, 1996, p. 23).

The impact that tax burdens have on growth rates is a controversial topic in empirical economics. The most detailed recent review of the evidence, most of it from American experience, finds that a reduction of 2·5 percentage points in the average tax rate (through a reduction of 5 percentage points in all marginal rates) would raise the growth rate by about 0·2 percentage points through its effects on accumulation and technological change (Engen and Skinner, 1996). An effect of this size might help explain why growth has slowed in Europe by more than in the UK since the Golden Age given the data in Table 5. Equally, however, such estimates also imply that the Conservatives' failure to make greater progress in reducing the welfare bill probably had a significant cost in terms of growth.

Table 8 makes clear that there has not been an increase in the share of investment in GDP – the UK remains below average in this area. On the other hand, there probably has been some improvement in the quality of investment given the rising proportion due to foreign direct investment (FDI) and the declining fraction under the auspices of nationalised industries. A recent econometric study found that FDI through its impact on technological change probably accounted for about 30 per cent of labour productivity growth in manufacturing between 1985 and 1995 (Barrell and Pain, 1997, p. 1,781).

The most difficult aspect of policy to assess is the impact of the extensive changes in education and training on human capital formation, productivity levels and growth. The general trend has clearly been one of rapid growth of investments both by firms and by persons. Real expenditures on training seem to have roughly trebled between 1971 and 1989, and the fraction of employees receiving job-related training in the last four weeks according to the Labour Force Survey rose from 8·5 per cent 1984 to 14·4 per cent in 1994 (Bean and Crafts, 1996). The take-up of opportunities provided by the state increased; whereas 47 per cent of 16-year-olds stayed on in full-time education in 1986, 10 years later this had risen to 71 per cent and the number of vocational qualifications obtained rose from 739,000 in 1990/1 to 912,000 in 1994/5 (Robinson, 1996). Broadberry and Wagner (1996, p. 258) report estimates that the proportion of managers who were graduates more than doubled between 1976 and 1986.

Table 8: Gross Non-Residential Investment
(per cent of GDP)

1960-1973		*1980-1989*		*1990-1995*	
Japan	26.5	Japan	23.4	Japan	24.7
Austria	21.1	Austria	18.5	Austria	19.0
Finland	20.0	Finland	18.3	Spain	17.3
Netherlands	19.8	Ireland	16.1	Germany	16.2
Germany	19.6	Spain	16.0	Netherlands	14.8
Spain	17.9	Italy	15.3	France	14.7
Sweden	16.8	Sweden	14.7	Belgium	14.1
Italy	16.6	France	14.6	Finland	13.9
Belgium	16.5	Netherlands	14.6	UK	13.2
Denmark	16.5	USA	14.5	Italy	13.1
France	16.3	Germany	14.3	Denmark	12.8
Ireland	16.1	Belgium	13.9	USA	12.6
UK	14.6	UK	13.8	Sweden	12.3
USA	13.5	Denmark	13.5	Ireland	11.8

Sources: OECD (1996a, 1997a).

On the other hand, there has been much criticism of the reforms of vocational training and of the continued deficiencies of the state school system with regard to the education of the less able. Critics note that the whole of the expansion in vocational qualifications has been at the bottom end of the hierarchy (Robinson, 1996) and that there is still a big deficit in the flow of qualified young workers relative to countries like Germany despite reductions in standards of assessment and breadth of knowledge (Steedman, 1997). Unfortunately, there exists no reliable quantification of the benefits of the policy reforms.

In principle, the best overall indicator for comparisons of productivity performance is TFP growth, although in practice measurement problems are often considerable. The endogenous growth models (discussed in Section 3) predict that, in the long run, growth will be proportional to TFP growth and will reflect incentives and opportunities for cost-reduction. Moreover, given their emphasis on increasing incentives rather than subsidising investment, this is an appropriate yardstick by which to judge the outcome of the Conservatives' strategy.

Table 9: Total Factor Productivity (TFP) Growth in the Business Sector
(per cent per year)

1960-73		*1979-95*	
Japan	5·4	Ireland	2·8
Ireland	4·6	Finland	2·6
Italy	4·4	Spain	1·6
Finland	4·0	UK	1·5
Belgium	3·8	France	1·3
France	3·7	Belgium	1·2
Netherlands	3·4	Denmark	1·2
Spain	3·2	Italy	1·1
Austria	3·1	Japan	1·1
Germany	2·6	Netherlands	1·1
UK	2·6	Sweden	1·1
USA	2·5	Austria	1·0
Denmark	2·3	Germany	0·6
Switzerland	2·1	USA	0·5
Norway	2·0	Norway	0·2
Sweden	2·0	Switzerland	-0·1

Source: OECD (1997a).

The estimates in Table 9 show that the UK moved up from 11th in 1960-73 to fourth in 1979-95 among these OECD countries. While TFP growth in the business sector slowed sharply in most OECD countries as catch-up growth petered out, the slowdown in the UK was much less severe. It is also encouraging to note that UK TFP growth since 1989 has been sustained at the same rate as for 1979-89, which argues against the suggestion that the relative strength of TFP growth is due to transitory factors. Indeed, Table 9 gives some reason to hope that economic decline relative to mainland Europe may have ceased or even now be capable of being reversed. It would, however, be easier to have confidence in this possibility had service sector productivity responded better to the Thatcher experiment.

Trends in NAIRU

The Conservative strategy to reduce NAIRU centred initially on reducing the adverse impacts of industrial relations and the benefit system. These were supplemented in the late 1980s by reforms to education and training intended to address the unskilled worker problem. The changes which ensued in the replacement ratio, the coverage of collective bargaining and the trade union differential were enough eventually to have a substantial effect on the NAIRU as the experience of the recent recovery tends to suggest.

Nickell (1997, p. 64) presents a regression to explain international unemployment levels and the estimated coefficients also support this view. Thus, the coverage of collective bargaining fell from 70 per cent to 47 per cent between 1980 and 1994 (OECD, 1997b) and the replacement rate fell by 20 percentage points from 1980 to 1990 (Melliss and Webb, 1997) which would be estimated to have an effect sufficient to reduce equilibrium unemployment by about 4 percentage points. Estimates of the NAIRU come with large confidence intervals and typically there is a distinction between the short and the long run (that is, when the labour market has completely adjusted). Melliss and Webb report that the Treasury's estimates show a sharp fall in the NAIRU to a short-run figure of 5-7 per cent and a long-run figure of 2-4 per cent (1997, pp. 34-35). The estimates in Table 10, which for 1995 are for the short run, also suggest some improvement in the UK's position relative to its peer group.

Nevertheless, there clearly were weaknesses in the strategy for reducing equilibrium unemployment. The most obvious was the failure to limit the duration of unemployment benefits prior to the introduction of the Jobseekers Allowance in 1996. The regression evidence presented by Nickell (1997) indicates that this was an important omission given the sizeable impact that it appears to have on unemployment. In addition, the introduction of the National Curriculum does not appear through 1995 to have reduced the problem of relatively low British attainments at the bottom end of

Table 10: Estimates of the NAIRU (per cent)

1960-1968		*1980-1988*		*1995*	
Switzerland	0·1	Switzerland	1·4	Japan	2·5
Germany	0·5	Japan	2·1	Switzerland	2·7
Austria	0·9	Sweden	2·4	Austria	4·1
Finland	1·4	Norway	2·5	Norway	5·1
Netherlands	1·5	Austria	3·0	USA	5·5
Japan	1·6	Germany	4·0	Sweden	6·6
Sweden	1·6	Finland	4·6	Netherlands	6·8
France	1·8	Italy	5·4	UK	7·0
Norway	2·1	USA	6·4	Germany	8·4
Denmark	2·2	Belgium	7·0	France	8·8
UK	2·6	Denmark	7·3	Italy	8·8
Belgium	3·8	Netherlands	7·3	Denmark	10·0
Italy	4·3	France	7·8	Belgium	10·8
Spain	4·6	UK	7·9	Ireland	13·6
USA	5·0	Ireland	13·1	Finland	14·8
Ireland	6·1	Spain	15·0	Spain	20·8

Sources: Layard *et al*. (1994) and, for 1995, OECD (1996b).

the education system, at least as far as the key subject of mathematics is concerned (Prais, 1997).

Finally, it should be recognised that restraints on public spending probably also had a pay-off in promoting the relative improvement in equilibrium unemployment in the UK. Table 5 shows that in the early 1990s current disbursements were around 12 per cent of GDP lower than the average of Western European countries. According to the Nickell equation, the taxes to finance this would have raised unemployment by about 2 percentage points.

Given the legacy of 1979 in terms of industrial relations, inefficient use of labour and low skills and the political difficulty of labour market reform, unemployment might have been a great deal worse. The Conservatives deserve more credit than they are usually allowed for averting that outcome.

7. Conclusions

The long period of Conservative government has left long-term growth prospects in Britain better than would have seemed possible 18 years ago and, combined with a slowdown in competitor countries, may even permit the reversal of relative economic decline *vis-à-vis* Europe in future. The relatively low level of equilibrium unemployment in Britain can also be seen as a success for the supply-side policies of the Conservatives, although continuing weaknesses in the education and training of the labour force have meant that this has had a less attractive counterpart in rising wage inequalities. Macro-economic management was clearly the Conservatives' Achilles' Heel, with major errors responsible for excessive economic fluctuations and the eventual loss of the government's reputation for economic competence, while at the same time the record on inflation compares unfavourably with that of other OECD countries.

While most of the governments' macro-economic gambles failed miserably, micro-economic radicalism paid off handsomely through privatisation, improved industrial relations, and de-coupling the UK from the European tendency to excessive government budgets. Nevertheless, opportunities to push through this agenda more fully were badly missed, notably in the areas of welfare and tax reforms, and the Conservatives' short-termism was frequently only too apparent.

A clear implication, as the Blairites have accepted, is that 'Old Labour' got it badly wrong in key areas of policy if macro-economic outcomes are the criteria by which to judge. In particular, their attachment to state ownership, protectionism, high taxation, subsidies to physical investment, and Keynesian demand management, together with unwillingness to accept reforms to industrial relations and welfare benefits, were most unfortunate. So, have 'New Labour' drawn the right lessons from the Conservatives' experience?

In important aspects, the early actions and rhetoric suggest that the answer is 'yes'. The establishment of an independent central bank, the obvious lack of interest in reversing privatisation, and continued restraint of public expenditure all provide evidence. The announced intentions to raise standards of education in bad state schools and to promote fundamental reform of welfare provision are encouraging, but it remains to be seen what will be achieved in these difficult areas. Whether 'New Labour' has really grasped the central rôle of incentives is less certain and the signals from their first Budget are rather mixed. Nevertheless, with its large majority and implicit acceptance that most of the supply-side reforms of the Conservative years were basically right, the new government has an excellent opportunity to complete the unfinished business and to raise the trend rate of growth a little more.

References

Aghion, P., and Howitt, P. (1997): 'A Schumpeterian Perspective on Growth and Competition', in D. M. Kreps and K. F. Wallis (eds.), *Advances in Economics and Econometrics*, Vol. II, Cambridge: Cambridge University Press, pp. 279-317.

Alesina, A., and Summers, L. H. (1993): 'Central Bank Independence and Macroeconomic Performance: Some Comparative Evidence', *Journal of Money, Credit and Banking*, Vol. 25, pp.151-62.

Alogoskoufis, G., Bean, C., Bertola, G., Cohen, D., Dolado, J., and Saint-Paul, G. (1995): *Unemployment: Choices for Europe*, London: Centre for Economic Policy Research.

Barrell, R., and Pain, N. (1997): 'Foreign Direct Investment, Technological Change and Economic Growth within Europe', *Economic Journal*, Vol. 107, pp. 1,770-86.

Bean, C. R. (1994): 'European Unemployment: A Survey', *Journal of Economic Literature*, Vol. 32, pp. 573-619.

Bean, C. R., and Crafts, N. F. R. (1996): 'British Economic Growth Since 1945: Relative Economic Decline...and Renaissance?', in N. F. R. Crafts and G. Toniolo (eds.), *Economic Growth in Europe Since 1945*, Cambridge: Cambridge University Press, pp. 131-72.

Bean, C. R. and Symons, J. (1989): 'Ten Years of Mrs T.', *NBER Macroeconomics Annual*, Vol. 3, pp. 13-61.

Bishop, M., and Thompson, D. (1992): 'Regulatory Reform and Productivity Growth in the UK's Public Utilities', *Applied Economics*, Vol. 24, pp. 1,181-90.

Bordo, M. D., and Kydland, F. E. (1995): 'The Gold Standard as a Rule: An Essay in Exploration', *Explorations in Economic History*, Vol. 32, pp. 423-64.

Britton, A. J. C. (1991): *Macroeconomic Policy in Britain, 1974-1987,* Cambridge: Cambridge University Press.

Broadberry, S. N., and Wagner, K. (1996): 'Human Capital and Productivity in Manufacturing during the Twentieth Century: Britain, Germany and the United States', in B. van Ark and N. F. R. Crafts (eds.), *Quantitative Aspects of Postwar European Economic Growth,* Cambridge: Cambridge University Press, pp. 244-70.

Crafts, N. F. R. (1996): 'Post-Neoclassical Endogenous Growth Theory: What are its Policy Implications?', *Oxford Review of Economic Policy,* Vol. 12(2), pp. 30-47.

Crafts, N. F. R. (1997): *Britain's Relative Economic Decline 1870-1995: A Quantitative Perspective,* London: Social Market Foundation.

Crafts, N. F. R., and Toniolo, G. (1996): 'Postwar Growth: An Overview', in N. F. R. Crafts and G. Toniolo (eds.), *Economic Growth in Europe since 1945,* Cambridge: Cambridge University Press, pp. 1-37.

Crouch, C. (1993): *Industrial Relations and European State Traditions,* Oxford: Clarendon Press.

Denny, K., and Nickell, S. (1992): 'Unions and Investment in British Industry', *Economic Journal,* Vol. 102, pp. 874-87.

Dilnot, A. W., Kay, J. A., and Morris, C. N. (1984): *The Reform of Social Security,* Oxford: Clarendon Press.

Dowrick, S. (1996): 'Estimating the Impact of Government Consumption on Growth: Growth Accounting and Endogenous Growth Models', in S. Durlauf, J. Helliwell and B. Raj (eds.), *Long Run Economic Growth,* Heidelberg: Physica-Verlag, pp. 163-84.

38

Edwards, S. (1997): 'Openness, Productivity and Growth: What Do We Really Know?', NBER Working Paper No. 5978.

Eichengreen, B., and Sachs, J. (1985): 'Exchange Rates and Economic Recovery in the 1930s', *Journal of Economic History*, Vol. 45, pp. 925-46.

Engen, E. M., and Skinner, J. (1996): 'Taxation and Economic Growth', NBER Working Paper No. 5826.

Fernandez, R., and Rodrik, D. (1991): 'Resistance to Reform: Status-Quo Bias in the Presence of Individual-Specific Uncertainty', *American Economic Review*, Vol. 81, pp. 1,146-55.

Haldane, A. G. (1995): 'Rules, Discretion and the United Kingdom's New Monetary Framework', Bank of England Working Paper No. 40.

Haskel, J. (1991): 'Imperfect Competition, Work Practices and Productivity Growth', *Oxford Bulletin of Economics and Statistics*, Vol. 53, pp. 265-79.

IFO (1997): *IFO Digest*, Munich.

Koedijk, K., and Kremers, J. (1996): 'Market Opening, Regulation and Growth in Europe', *Economic Policy*, Vol. 23, pp. 445-67.

Layard, R., and Nickell, S. (1985): 'The Causes of British Unemployment', *National Institute Economic Review*, No. 111, pp. 62-85.

Layard, R., Nickell, S., and Jackman, R. (1994): *The Unemployment Crisis*, Oxford: Oxford University Press.

Maddison, A. (1995): *Monitoring the World Economy, 1820-1992*, Paris: OECD.

Maddison, A. (1997): *The Nature and Functioning of European Capitalism: A Historical and Comparative Perspective*, Groningen: Growth and Development Centre.

Melliss, C., and Webb, A. E. (1997): 'The UK NAIRU: Concepts, Measurement and Policy Implications', OECD Working Paper No. 78.

Newbery, D. M., and Pollitt, M. G. (1996): 'The Restructuring and Privatisation of the CEGB: Was It Worth It?', University of Cambridge DAE Working Paper No. 9607.

Nickell, S. (1997): 'Unemployment and Labor Market Rigidities: Europe versus North America', *Journal of Economic Perspectives*, Vol. 11(3), pp. 55-74.

Nickell, S., and Bell, B. (1996): 'Changes in the Distribution of Wages and Unemployment in OECD Countries', *American Economic Review Papers and Proceedings*, Vol. 86, pp. 302-08.

Nickell, S., Wadhwani, S., and Wall, M. (1992): 'Productivity Growth in UK Companies, 1975-1986', *European Economic Review*, Vol. 36, pp. 1,055-85.

OECD (1996a): *Historical Statistics, 1960-1994*, Paris: OECD.

OECD (1996b): *Employment Outlook*, Paris: OECD.

OECD (1997a): *Economic Outlook*, Paris: OECD.

OECD (1997b): *Employment Outlook*, Paris: OECD.

ONS: Office of National Statistics (1997): *Economic Trends Annual Supplement*, London.

O'Mahony, M., Oulton, N., and Voss, J. (1996): 'Productivity in Market Services: International Comparisons', London: National Institute of Economic and Social Research Discussion Paper No. 105.

O'Mahony, M., and Wagner, K. (1994): *Changing Fortunes: An Industry Study of British and German Productivity Growth over Three Decades*, London: NIESR.

Oulton, N. (1995): 'Supply-Side Reform and UK Economic Growth: What Happened to the Miracle?', *National Institute Economic Review*, No. 154, pp. 53-69.

Oulton, N., and Young, G. (1996): 'How High is the Social Rate of Return to Investment?', *Oxford Review of Economic Policy*, Vol. 12(2), pp. 48-69.

Owens, J., and Whitehouse, E. (1996): 'Tax Reform for the 21st Century', *Bulletin for International Fiscal Documentation*, Vol. 50, pp. 538-47.

Parker, D., and Martin, S. (1995): 'The Impact of UK Privatisation on Labour and Total Factor Productivity', *Scottish Journal of Political Economy*, Vol. 42, pp. 201-20.

Pilat, D. (1996): 'Labour Productivity Levels in OECD Countries', OECD Working Paper No. 169.

Prais, S. J. (1981): *Productivity and Industrial Structure*, Cambridge: Cambridge University Press.

Prais, S. J. (1997): 'How Did English Schools and Pupils *Really* Perform in the 1995 International Comparisons in Mathematics?', *National Institute Economic Review*, No. 161, pp. 53-68.

Pratten, C. F., and Atkinson, A. G. (1976): 'The Use of Manpower in British Industry', *Department of Employment Gazette*, Vol. 84, pp. 571-76.

Robinson, P. (1996): *Rhetoric and Reality: Britain's New Vocational Qualifications*, London: Centre for Economic Performance, London School of Economics.

Singh, A. (1975): 'Takeovers, Natural Selection and the Theory of the Firm: Evidence from the Postwar UK Experience', *Economic Journal*, Vol. 85, pp. 497-515.

Soskice, D. (1994): 'Reconciling Markets and Institutions: The German Apprenticeship System', in L. M. Lynch (ed.), *Training and the Private Sector: International Comparisons*, Chicago: University of Chicago Press, pp. 25-60.

Statistisches Bundesamt (1997): *Statistisches Jahrbuch*, Wiesbaden.

Steedman, H. (1990): 'Improvement in Workforce Qualifications: Britain and France, 1979-88', *National Institute Economic Review*, No. 133, pp. 50-61.

Steedman, H. (1997): 'Recent Trends in Engineering and Construction Skill Formation – UK and Germany Compared', Centre for Economic Performance, LSE, Discussion Paper No.353.

Tyrie, A. (1996): *The Prospects for Public Spending*, London: Social Market Foundation.

van Ark, B. (1993): *International Comparisons of Output and Productivity*, Groningen: Growth and Development Centre.

Vickers, J., and Yarrow, G. (1988): *Privatization: An Economic Analysis,* Cambridge, Mass.: MIT Press.

Walsh, C. (1995): 'Is New Zealand's Reserve Bank Act of 1989 an Optimal Central Bank Contract?', *Journal of Money, Credit and Banking,* Vol. 27, pp. 1,179-91.

Williams, M. E. (1993): 'The Effectiveness of Competition Policy in the UK', *Oxford Review of Economic Policy*, Vol. 9(2), pp. 94-112.

The Wincott Memorial Lectures

1. **The Counter-Revolution in Monetary Theory**
   MILTON FRIEDMAN
   1970 *Occasional Paper 33* 5th Impression 1983 £1.00

2. **Wages and Prices in a Mixed Economy**
   JAMES E. MEADE
   1971 *Occasional Paper 35* Out of print

3. **Government and High Technology**
   JOHN JEWKES
   1972 *Occasional Paper 37* Out of print

4. **Economic Freedom and Representative Government**
   F.A.HAYEK
   1973 *Occasional Paper 39* 3rd Impression 1980 Out of print

5. **Aspects of Post-war Economic Policy**
   LORD ROBBINS
   1974 *Occasional Paper 42* £1.00

6. **A General Hypothesis of Employment, Inflation and Politics**
   PETER JAY
   1976 *Occasional Paper 46* 2nd Impression 1977 £1.00

7. **The Credibility of Liberal Economics**
   ALAN PEACOCK
   1977 *Occasional Paper 50* Out of print

8. **Economists and the British Economy**
   ALAN WALTERS
   1978 *Occasional Paper 54* £1.00

9. **Choice in European Monetary Union**
   ROLAND VAUBEL
   1979 *Occasional Paper 55* £1.00

10. **Whatever Happened to Productivity?**
    GRAHAM HUTTON
    1980 *Occasional Paper 56* Out of print

Democratic Values and the Currency

Michael Portillo

with a Postscript by
Martin Feldstein

1. The single currency is not 'merely an economic device' but '…a project in re-shaping the way our Continent is governed'.
2. The 'federalism' now being pursued at European level is 'highly centralising and owes much to the Monnet-functionalist approach'.
3. Much of the momentum behind European integration derives from the fear of war. But Europe is more secure from inter-continental conflict than ever before because it is composed of democracies and '…it is inconceivable that democracies would go to war with one another'.
4. European integration is '…not the means to achieve the security of our Continent'. Because the form of integration reduces democratic control, rather than abolishing nationalism it risks stirring it up.
5. For democracy to work, people have to have more than just a vote. Resentment and unrest will be the result if policies are made by bodies '…thought to be too distant, or made by people who are not democratically accountable at all'.
6. Motivation for the single currency is political, not economic. It is '…a bigger step towards centralised decision-making than any that has been taken before'
7. Monetary policy will become the responsibility of a European Union central bank. Constraints on borrowing will restrict member-countries' freedom to decide either tax rates or spending levels. Because there is no single labour market, and the flexibility of currency adjustment will have been lost, the '…full impact of recession will …fall on unemployment'.
8. Electors will feel 'resentful and cheated' when they cannot through their votes influence economic policy or change the policy-makers.
9. Trying to establish democratic accountability at European level is not the answer. 'Europe' does not constitute a nation. 'No parliament spanning from Dublin to Athens …is capable of satisfying the democratic requirements and aspirations of each of our populations'.
10. Though the EU is composed of democracies, the Union itself is undemocratic. Transferring decisions from member-states to the Union reduces democratic accountability with the danger of providing '…a breeding ground for nationalism and extremism'.

The Institute of Economic Affairs

2 Lord North Street, Westminster, London SW1P 3LB
Telephone: 0171 799 3745 Facsimile: 0171 799 2137
E-mail: iea@iea.org.uk Internet: http://www.iea.org.uk

£4.00

ISBN 0-255 36412-1